LEGACIES OF JESUS

LEGACIES OF JESUS

LOWELL L. BENNION

Deseret Book Company
Salt Lake City, Utah

Library of Congress Cataloging-in-Publication Data

Bennion, Lowell Lindsay, 1908–
    Legacies of Jesus / by Lowell L. Bennion.
       p. cm.
    Includes index.
    ISBN 0-87579-361-4
    1. Jesus Christ — Person and offices. 2. Bennion, Lowell Lindsay,
1980 —   . I. Title.
BT202.B366   1990
232 — dc20   90-39169
                                       CIP

Printed in the United States of America

10   9   8   7   6   5   4   3   2   1

Contents

Preface   *vii*

1   Jesus the Emissary and Examplar   *1*

2   Jesus the Humanitarian   *9*

3   Jesus' Sense of Values   *17*

4   Four Essential Teachings of Jesus   *23*

5   Jesus' Art of Teaching   *49*

6   Jesus and the Atonement   *57*

Preface

Few who have ever lived can equal Jesus of Nazareth in the extent and diversity of his appeal to the people living since his day. Radical feminists and unreconstructed patriarchs, skeptical scholars and those who read the scriptures as totally literal, sinners and saints, rich and poor, revolutionaries and conservatives are drawn to him. Architects, painters, composers, and writers have found in his life and teachings the inspiration for countless works of art.

In this brief work, I explore some of the reasons for his great appeal to me. I cannot do justice to his life or teachings. I cannot argue in a scholarly way for a particular point of view. Rather, I write to express my intense gratitude for what he has come to mean to me. In quiet ways, throughout my life, I have sensed what I hope is a growing closeness to him. As my life draws toward its close, I find myself thinking of him, not only with the love of a lifetime but also with the anticipation of my future.

I hope that I may encourage others to know Jesus better.

Acknowledgments

My son Ben, my wife Merle, Emma Lou Thayne, and Laurie Di Pavoda have read the manuscript in the making and made helpful suggestions and lent encouragement. Lavina Fielding Anderson did a careful editing of the entire manuscript, contributing much to both the content and form of the work. I appreciate their fine contributions. I take full responsibility for points of view expressed and the manuscript's limitations.

Chapter 1

Jesus the Emissary and Exemplar

History has seen two distinct types of religious leaders: emissaries and exemplars. Although both men and women have provided leadership and inspiration of both kinds, this discussion is drawn primarily from the Old and New Testaments, whose examples deal primarily with men. A discussion of women in these roles lies outside the scope of this particular essay, and masculine nouns and pronouns are used for that reason.

Emissaries are individuals who feel that God has personally called them to bear his word and will to the people. They demand to

be listened to—not for their own sakes but
because they are messengers of Deity. The pro-
totypes of emissary prophets in Israel include
Moses, Samuel, Elijah, and the great literary
prophets, such as Amos, Hosea, Micah, Jere-
miah, Isaiah, and Ezekiel.

What kind of men were they? They were
dynamic, audacious, emotionally intense, and
passionately absorbed by the quality of their
people's lives and the fate of their nation. They
made no claim to personal perfection. Their
message was not "Do as I do," but rather "Do
as the Lord commands you." They frequently
suffered rejection, persecution, and even mar-
tyrdom at the hands of their people. More pain-
fully, they were wounded by the also frequent
failure of their people to catch fire from the
burning words they had received from the
Lord.

Their messages are among the most eloquent that have come to us from the ancient
world. Frequently, they were scathing in their
rebuke of their followers' sloth and sin. Amos,
for example, a shepherd from the hills of Judea
and the southern kingdom of Judah, went to
Bethel, a shrine city in the northern kingdom

of Israel. In the name of God, he condemned their injustice and lack of human mercy. Amaziah, priest of Bethel, correctly heard this rebuke as an attack on the house of Israel:

"Then Amaziah the priest of Bethel sent to Jeroboam king of Israel, saying, Amos hath conspired against thee in the midst of the house of Israel: the land is not able to bear all his words. For thus Amos saith, Jeroboam shall die by the sword, and Israel shall surely be led away captive out of their own land.

"Also Amaziah said unto Amos, O thou seer, go, flee thee away into the land of Judah, and there eat bread, and prophesy there: But prophesy not again any more at Bethel: for it is the king's chapel, and it is the king's court.

"Then answered Amos, and said to Amaziah, I was no prophet, neither was I a prophet's son; but I was an herdman, and a gatherer of sycomore fruit:

"And the Lord took me as I followed the flock, and the Lord said unto me, Go, prophesy unto my people Israel. Now therefore hear thou the word of the Lord." (Amos 7:10–16.)

These emissary prophets have been called God-intoxicated men because they spoke for him in the first person and with irresistible confidence.

In contrast are the exemplars, who include such men of the Far East as Buddha, Confucius, Lao-tze, Mahvira, and Hindu gurus. They did not speak for God; in fact, some, like Confucius and Buddha, were likely agnostic. Rather, they spoke about human problems with an inspired wisdom that sought human solutions among the best qualities of human beings — tolerance, love, compassion, and reason.

Each of these men developed a distinctive interpretation of life and recommended certain habits of living that would put individuals in harmony with the forces of life. Above all, they were ethicists who, by both precept and example, drew other human beings to lead better lives. In contrast to the aggressive combativeness with which the emissary prophets denounced and derided the political and social conditions of their day, the exemplars reflected on universal themes of human experience and pronounced universally true precepts that would help human beings understand their own experience and live more profoundly.

I have long been impressed by the remarkable fact that Jesus alone, among the founders of the world religions, was both an emissary and an exemplar. Like his fellow Israelites, he announced himself as an emissary. He repeatedly acknowledged that he had been sent from the Father, taught the teachings of the Father, and pointed the worship of others in the direction of the Father.

To the man who asked, "Good Master, what shall I do that I may inherit eternal life?" Jesus replied, *"Why callest thou me good? there is none good but one, that is, God."* (Mark 10: 17–18.)

When Jesus was in the temple, the Jews marveled and asked, "How knoweth this man letters, never having learned?" And Jesus answered: *"My doctrine is not mine, but his that sent me. If any man will do his will, he shall know of the doctrine, whether it be of God, or whether I speak of myself. He that speaketh of himself seeketh his own glory: but he that seeketh his glory that sent him, the same is true, and no unrighteousness is in him."* (John 7:14–18.)

On other occasions Jesus taught:

"My meat is to do the will of him that sent me, and to finish his work." (John 4:34.)

"Verily, verily, I say unto you, The Son can do nothing of himself, but what he seeth the Father do: for what things soever he doeth, these also doeth the Son likewise." (John 5:19.)

"I can of mine own self do nothing: as I hear, I judge: and my judgment is just; because I seek not mine own will, but the will of the Father which hath sent me." (John 5:30.)

Yet Jesus was simultaneously an exemplar, inviting people to come unto him to find peace and salvation and to follow his way of life. He declared:

"Come unto me, all ye that labour and are heavy laden, and I will give you rest. Take my yoke upon you, and learn of me; for I am meek and lowly in heart: and ye shall find rest unto your souls. For my yoke is easy, and my burden is light." (Matthew 11:28–30.)

"I am the bread of life: he that cometh to me shall never hunger; and he that believeth on me shall never thirst. . . . I am the living bread which came down from heaven: if any man eat of this bread, he shall live for ever: and the bread that I will give is my flesh, which I will give for the life of the world." (John 6:35, 51.)

"I am the way, the truth, and the life: no man cometh unto the Father, but by me. If ye had known me, ye should have known my Father also: and from henceforth ye know him, and have seen him." (John 14:6.)

When one of the disciples, Philip, commented, "Lord, shew us the Father, and it sufficeth us," Jesus responded:

"Have I been so long time with you, and yet hast thou not known me, Philip? he that hath seen me hath seen the Father; and how sayest thou then, shew us the Father?" (John 14:8–9.)

We can follow Jesus because we believe that he speaks and acts for God and that in his word we are hearing the will of God for us. Or we can follow him because his teachings and character show us an ideal of humanity at its highest.

In the course of my life, I have felt both the power of his authority and the inspiration of his example. Both draw me upward, one toward a vision of redeemed humankind in which I can participate, and the other toward the serious but joyful work of better realizing my human potential. Both of these attributes are potent, both as idea and as ideal. I fully and deeply acknowledge Jesus' claim to be both emissary and exemplar, and I honor him in both roles.

Chapter 2

Jesus the Humanitarian

Jesus was no closet philosopher. As we read
through the record of his life in the New Testament, we discover how freely he mingled
with a rich variety of people and how consis-
tently positive those interactions were. He went
about doing good; where he had passed, the
blind saw, the deaf heard, the dumb spoke, the
crippled walked, and the mentally disturbed
were free of oppression. Multitudes followed
him, seeing his wondrous works and hearing
his words.

Jesus spoke to innumerable large groups
with inspired power, and miraculously fed
multitudes, but we primarily see him dealing

with individuals, sensitive to individual needs. The classic example is the woman who made her way through the crowd that surrounded him to touch the hem of his garment, thus finding healing from an affliction she had had for twelve years. She had spent her last farthing on physicians, exhausting the ability of human wisdom to help her. Sensing her, Jesus immediately asked who had touched him. "Thou seest the multitude thronging thee," protested his disciples, "and sayest thou, Who touched me?" But Jesus insisted that someone had done so, for virtue, or strength, had left him. (See Mark 5:24–34.)

In that story, we find faith that our own need, however desperate, and our own faith, however flawed, will also be perceived by the being we revere as our Savior.

In the patriarchal society of Jesus' day, women and children were valued less than men. Mothers brought little children to him, seeking a blessing for them. Again, the less sensitive disciples scolded them and shooed them away, no doubt thinking that Jesus should not be bothered by these demands. But his response was, *"Suffer the little children to come unto me, and forbid them not: for of such is the kingdom of God.*" He then used the incident to teach a valuable lesson on humility: "*Whosoever shall not receive the kingdom of God as a little child, he shall not enter therein.*" (Mark 10:13–15.) Holding this example in mind can provide a counterbalance to the pressures of society when we must decide which people are "important" and which are not.

Condemned sinners and lepers were the most alienated members of Jewish society. To test Jesus and find cause for punishing him, scribes and Pharisees brought before him, as he taught in the temple, a woman who they said had been "taken in adultery, in the very act." Then they cannily asked, "Now Moses in the law commanded us, that such should be stoned: but what sayest thou?"

Jesus responded, "*He that is without sin among you, let him first cast a stone at her.*"

They slunk away one by one, "convicted by their own conscience," until Jesus and the woman were alone.

"*Woman,*" he asked, "*where are those thine accusers? hath no man condemned thee?*" When she answered "No man, Lord," Jesus told

her, *"Neither do I condemn thee: go, and sin
no more."* (John 8:3–11.)

Certainly Jesus did not condone adultery.
He strengthened the law of Moses by saying,
*"Whosoever looketh on a woman to lust after
her hath committed adultery with her already
in his heart."* (Matthew 5:28.) Yet in these circumstances, when men had already shamed
this woman, Jesus put her welfare above the
law, giving her hope through his kindness.

His words of forgiveness rise in my mind
when occasions to judge, criticize, and accuse
present themselves. As I have grown older, I
have less confidence in the persuasive power
of preaching and pointing out faults. It has been
my experience that most people — even rebellious teenagers, negligent parents, and slothful
public servants — do not really need to be re-
minded of the "shoulds" and "oughts" in their
lives. Rather than knowing better, they need
help in doing better. I cherish those occasions
when their repentance can begin with an act
of forgiveness rather than an act of judgment,
and I hope for myself the same charity from
the One whose right it is to judge.

On another occasion, sinners and publicans

drew near "for to hear him," a remarkable occurrence, since we would not usually think of sinners as comfortable in the presence of a person as pure as Jesus. The "Pharisees and scribes murmured, saying, This man receiveth sinners, and eateth with them." (Luke 15:1–2). Jesus responded by telling three remarkable parables: the lost sheep, the lost coin, and the lost son (the prodigal son). All three taught the worth of souls.

The parable of the prodigal son is a personal favorite of mine, for its beautiful image of the father's love for the sinner. As Jesus told the tale, the father did not simply accept his son's return but ran out to meet him. (See Luke 15:11–32.) Few scriptures so poignantly teach us how to allow others to change and how to welcome that change without trying to punish them or make them pay for their past mistakes.

Frequently, Jesus healed people on the Sabbath, much to the consternation of the scribes and Pharisees who knew that these acts of mercy violated the elaborate, oral laws regarding the Sabbath. In response to their criticism, he simply cut through to the important, underlying principle: *"I will ask you one thing; Is it lawful on the sabbath days to do good, or to do evil? to save life, or to destroy it?"* (Luke 6:9.)

As a people who cherish the laws of God and take seriously our responsibility to obey the laws of the land, it is well for us to remember that Jesus interpreted the law in a way that blessed human beings, not as something unrelated to life or as an end to be served in itself, but as an instrument of service.

Jesus was not always kind and gentle. He said what people needed to hear, so at times he was searing in his criticism. He upset the tables of the money changers, accusing them of turning a "house of prayer" into "a den of thieves." (Luke 19:46.) An entire chapter of Matthew reports Jesus' rejection of the pharisaic view of religion, illustrated particularly well by one verse: *"Woe unto you, scribes and Pharisees, hypocrites! for ye pay tithe of mint and anise and cummin, and have omitted the weightier matters of the law, judgment, mercy, and faith: these ought ye to have done, and not to leave the other undone."* (Matthew 23:23.)

In reading the Gospels, especially Matthew and Luke, it is fascinating to concentrate on

Jesus' relationship to people, including his chosen disciples. He showed respect and consideration for Peter, who was valiant and loyal in his discipleship. However, he also saw Peter's weaknesses and accurately predicted that the apostle would deny him thrice. When, out of a misplaced sense of protectiveness, Peter tried to dissuade the Lord from his mission, Jesus' rebuke, *"Get thee behind me, Satan"* (Matthew 16:23), must have shocked him into rethinking what he knew about this man.

Humanitarian causes have experienced various degrees of popularity in our culture for the past century. Much of the inspiration for humanitarian efforts has come from the example of Jesus, suffering and rejoicing with his fellow human beings, exerting himself on their behalf, and bringing to his task a sensitive understanding of their deep needs.

As a Latter-day Saint, I appreciate the record and current achievements of the Church in humanitarian efforts. I support these efforts and rejoice in our collective achievements. For me, four aspects of religion are significant, and these efforts represent one of those aspects: the Church, ordinances and rituals, religious and ethical principles, and a religious orientation toward other human beings. But the most important of the four is other people — what happens to individuals as the result of a religion. The Church is not an end in itself, but a means of making gospel principles like faith and humility functional in the lives of people. Yes, even gospel principles are not the things of ultimate worth. Their value lies in how they bless human lives.

Jesus has taught me to place individuals first and to keep them there. The Church and gospel principles then become wonderful ways to bless their lives — and mine.

Chapter 3

Jesus' Sense of Values

The message that seems to dominate the New Testament is the value Jesus placed on individuals. I believe it would be hard to go wrong if our priorities match his. But sometimes we don't know what is best for a person in a particular circumstance. How did Jesus know when to forgive and when to chasten? How can we learn when to serve and when to let another serve? In facing such questions, it helps to think about the fundamental values that shaped Jesus' own life. What did he identify as the purpose of life and what activities for him were of prime importance?

He answered these questions this way: *"I*

am come that they might have life, and that they might have it more abundantly." (John 10:10.) And what, for him, was the abundant life? Part of the answer is found in the Sermon on the Mount, which is a strongly antimaterialistic statement:

"Lay not up for yourselves treasures upon earth, where moth and rust doth corrupt, and where thieves break through and steal: but lay up for yourselves treasures in heaven, where neither moth nor rust doth corrupt, and where thieves do not break through nor steal. . . .

"No man can serve two masters: for either he will hate the one, and love the other; or else he will hold to the one, and despise the other. Ye cannot serve God and mammon. Therefore I say unto you, take no thought for your life, what ye shall eat, or what ye shall drink; nor yet for your body, what ye shall put on. Is not the life more than meat, and the body than raiment? . . .

"But seek ye first the kingdom of God, and his righteousness; and all these things shall be added unto you." (Matthew 6:19–20, 24–25, 33.)

Thus, the value he proclaimed to the multitude on the mount, a message that still speaks with living words to us today, is not to place our greatest effort on multiplying our material possessions, for *"the kingdom of God is within you."* (Luke 17:21.) Our well-being lies largely in our own state of mind and heart, in our own sense of worth, in our relationship with our fellow human beings, on finding meaning, and in experiencing joy. Jesus' teachings and way of life are a pathway to finding satisfaction in living.

The treasures of heaven Jesus speaks of are also the greatest treasures on earth. His true followers still possess these treasures. Alma celebrates the fruits of gospel living: "And because of your diligence and your faith and your patience with the word in nourishing it, that it may take root in you, behold, by and by ye shall pluck the fruit thereof, which is most precious, which is sweet above all that is sweet, and which is white above all that is white, yea, and pure above all that is pure; and ye shall feast upon this fruit even until ye are filled, that ye hunger not, neither shall ye thirst." (Alma 32:42.)

Jesus not only pointed out the path we

should follow, but also designated the path we should avoid, one that would lead to meaninglessness and isolate us increasingly within our own selfish circle. To a group that included his disciples, he explained:

"Whosoever will come after me, let him deny himself, and take up his cross, and follow me. For whosoever will save his life shall lose it; but whosoever shall lose his life for my sake and the gospel's, the same shall save it.

"For what shall it profit a man, if he shall gain the whole world, and lose his own soul? Or what shall a man give in exchange for his soul?

"Whosoever therefore shall be ashamed of me and of my words in this adulterous and sinful generation; of him also shall the Son of man be ashamed, when he cometh in the glory of his Father with the holy angels." (Mark 8:34–38.)

One of my students once shared with the class the experience of a widow in her hometown in Idaho. The woman's only child, a son, was killed in World War II, and she grieved inconsolably for both her son and herself and became ill.

Her doctor, a Latter-day Saint, found nothing medically wrong with her and treated her with placebos for a time, but she did not improve. One day he told her bluntly, "If you don't change your thinking and attitude of self-pity, you will become a burden to yourself and to this community. Do you believe in the gospel of Jesus Christ?"

Startled, she answered, "Of course I do."

"Then you had better start living it," said the exasperated doctor. "Get interested in other people. Visit elderly widows and shut-ins. Help some young mothers in need of assistance. Forget your own problems and serve others."

His call to repentance was salutary. The widow, after her shock subsided, took his advice to heart and discovered a kind of happiness she had never known before, not even when she had her family about her.

I would not be so bold as to claim that I have perfected this single-minded manner of living, but even my limited experience corroborates that the abundant *life* cannot be equated with an abundance of *things*.

The abundant life is the fulfilled life, one that is fully engaged with mind and heart, reaching out to the world around us and to the people in it, and living by faith in its divine origin and purpose.

Four Essential Teachings of Jesus

Not everything Jesus taught was new. Many of his ideas can be found in the Old Testament, and many others have parallels in the teachings of philosophers and the founders of other world religions.

When a lawyer asked Jesus, "Master, which is the great commandment in the law?" Jesus answered with a statement that should already have been very familiar to the lawyer:

"Thou shalt love the Lord thy God with all thy heart, and with all thy soul, and with all thy mind. This is the first and great commandment. And the second is like unto it, Thou shalt

love thy neighbour as thyself. On these two com-
mandments hang all the law and the prophets."
(Matthew 22:36–40.)

Jesus did not invent this principle. Love of
God was basic in the law of Moses: "Thou shalt
love the Lord thy God with all thine heart, and
with all thy soul, and with all thy might." (Deu-
teronomy 6:5.) The law of Moses also contains
an injunction to love one's neighbor: "Thou
shalt not avenge, nor bear any grudge against
the children of thy people, but thou shalt love
thy neighbour as thyself: I am the Lord." (Le-
viticus 19:18.)

Jesus' contribution was to bring these two
commandments together, quoting them sep-
arately but showing their relationship to each
other and also, as he so often did, showing
how the whole of religion stems from love for
God and love for our fellow human beings.

I do not insist on innovation and novelty
to make his teachings profound and powerful
for me, for what is unique about Jesus' teaching
is his emphasis and his wonderful art. He taught
principles more than rules, principles that support and enrich one another, principles so fun-

damental and universal in application that they have meaning in all ages and circumstances.

In science, isolated facts derive their meaning from basic principles and law. The same is true in religion. Individual rules, such as lists of activities that are permitted on the Sabbath and those that are forbidden, have little value unless they are related to the basic principle of the Sabbath — that its purpose is to help us draw nearer to God and to heal or bless other human beings. I marvel at his ability to deal so profoundly with underlying principles, applying them accurately to a wide range of diverse circumstances. Surely this is wisdom!

It has been my experience from time to time to meet individuals who are preoccupied with rules. They learn new rules eagerly and strive earnestly to keep every rule they know. I grieve for them. Despite their sincerity and earnest desires for righteousness (for which they will justly and meritoriously be rewarded), they have no concept of the creative, adventurous experience that living by principle can be. Such rigidity cannot endure long against the shocks of daily living, and sometimes the rule-bound individual breaks instead of learning flexibility. Surely that is not the direction of life toward which Jesus calls us.

Four principles that Jesus repeatedly emphasized are very dear to me. I would go so far as to argue that much of his essential thought is comprised in these principles: humility, integrity, love, and faith.

Humility

In the Beatitudes at the beginning of the Sermon on the Mount, Jesus names eight conditions of the mind and heart that bring the blessed state of happiness to an individual. The first of these, rendered in the King James Version as *"Blessed are the poor in spirit"* (Matthew 5:3), has traditionally been interpreted to mean those who are humble. Other translations express this beatitude as *"Blessed are they who feel their spiritual need"* and *"How blest are those who know their need of God."* Another meaning of this first beatitude, I believe, is that the meek are those who are teachable and open-minded, those who will learn from their fellow human beings as well as from God — not because it is the intellectually correct thing to do, but because they are not concerned with themselves and can truly listen and, therefore, learn. I have perhaps a rather unorthodox view of the humble as those who feel no need to continually take their personal pulse, analyze how they feel about a given topic, or develop and express an opinion on every item of conversation.

Some of us have mistakenly identified humility with stage fright. I believe that this condition, sympathetic though I am to the sufferer, is actually the opposite of humility because it is based on self-concern. The Chinese call it a fear of "losing face." It is truly a blessing to still the chatter and fretting of the ego with its constant worries, anxieties, and fidgeting. A preoccupation with almost anyone or anything — whether it be a baby, a loved one, a Bach cantata, or even a stamp collection — confers a very real kind of happiness that comes only with the ability to relate totally and unselfconsciously to someone or something else. The only preoccupation for which this is not true, in my opinion, is a preoccupation with the self.

Jesus has much to say and demonstrate about humility. Repeatedly he pointed out that persons of humility have no need to seek for worldly honor, put themselves forward, or anxiously claim their due. James and John, the sons of Zebedee, once asked Jesus for a special favor (rather slyly prefacing it with the request "that thou shouldest do for us whatsoever we shall desire"!), requesting the privilege of sitting "one on thy right hand, and the other on thy left hand" when he returned in his "glory." The other apostles were, naturally, "much displeased" with James and John, but Jesus took the occasion to teach them all a lesson about humility:

"Ye know that they which are accounted to rule over the Gentiles exercise lordship over them; and their great ones exercise authority upon them. But so shall it not be among you: but whosoever will be great among you, shall be your minister: and whosoever of you will be the chiefest, shall be servant of all. For even the Son of man came not to be ministered unto, but to minister, and to give his life a ransom for many." (See Mark 10:35–45.)

Those who are humble feel no need to seek for worldly honors or recognition. Rather, they focus on the needs and well-being of others.

My father, Milton Bennion, was dean of the

College of Education at the University of Utah
for over thirty years. Three of his colleagues,
appointed by him, told me on separate occasions how he had gone out of his way to pro-
mote their professional status and ensure their
success when he could easily have garnered
honors or taken credit for himself. I believe
that he had learned from Jesus to rejoice in
the achievements of others.

Jesus returned to the concept of humility
in an interesting parable aimed directly at certain individuals who "trusted in themselves that
they were righteous, and despised others." He
taught them:

*"Two men went up into the temple to pray;
the one a Pharisee, and the other a publican.
The Pharisee stood and prayed thus with himself, God, I thank thee, that I am not as other
men are, extortioners, unjust, adulterers, or
even as this publican. I fast twice in the week,
I give tithes of all that I possess. And the publican, standing afar off, would not lift up so
much as his eyes unto heaven, but smote upon
his breast, saying, God be merciful to me a
sinner. I tell you, this man went down to his
house justified rather than the other: for every*

one that exalteth himself shall be abased; and he that humbleth himself shall be exalted." (Luke 18:9–14.)

It is appropriate that humility should be the first beatitude because it is a prerequisite to the beatitudes that follow. Humble people recognize and regret their sins and mistakes; they are meek, gentle, peaceable, and self-controlled. Certainly they hunger and thirst after righteousness and truth. The last four beatitudes are expressions of love, and we cannot love others if we are arrogant or self-centered.

In another important passage, Jesus taught about humility when his disciples showed an interest in rank and hierarchy and asked, "Who is the greatest in the kingdom of heaven?"

In response, we are told that Jesus called a little child to him, set him in the midst of them, and declared, *"Verily I say unto you, Except ye be converted, and become as little children, ye shall not enter into the kingdom of heaven. Whosoever therefore shall humble himself as this little child, the same is greatest in the kingdom of heaven."* (Matthew 18:1–4.)

In what sense did Jesus call the child humble? I believe that he wanted to emphasize to the apostles the difference between the child's openness and his acceptance of what was happening at that very moment. The scriptural account does not tell us what the child was doing when Jesus called him over. Was he listening to the conversation, playing a game with other children, or even running an errand? It did not matter. He responded immediately to Jesus' call and allowed himself to be "set in the midst of them" without demur. The concreteness and actuality of the child's experience contrasts sharply with the apostles' preoccupation with — and disputes over — a future state upon which they had no information but which was blocking their ability to experience the presence of the living Christ.

Those who are humble also recognize that they do not have a full knowledge of any principle of the gospel. They understand that faith, repentance, and love are words with profound meanings and implications. They keep their minds open for new insights and ponder their experience for new understandings. With Isaiah, they recognize the difference between their understanding and that of Deity:

"Seek ye the Lord while he may be found,

call ye upon him while he is near: Let the wicked forsake his way, and the unrighteous man his thoughts: and let him return unto the Lord, and he will have mercy upon him; and to our God, for he will abundantly pardon. *For my thoughts are not your thoughts, neither are your ways my ways,* saith the Lord. *For as the heavens are higher than the earth, so are my ways higher than your ways, and my thoughts than your thoughts.*" (Isaiah 55:6–9.)

Jesus reinforced the importance of being teachable by admonishing believers: *"Ask, and it shall be given you; seek, and ye shall find; knock, and it shall be opened unto you: For every one that asketh receiveth; and he that seeketh findeth; and to him that knocketh it shall be opened."* (Matthew 7:7–8.)

To those Jews who believed on him, he declared, *"If ye continue in my word, then are ye my disciples indeed; and ye shall know the truth, and the truth shall make you free."* (John 8:31–32.)

The Book of Mormon prophet Alma makes a fine distinction between humility that comes from being compelled to be humble by external circumstances like poverty, and humility that comes as the fruit of believing in the word of God:

"I say unto you, it is well that ye are cast out of your synagogues, that ye may be humble, and that ye may learn wisdom; for it is necessary that ye should learn wisdom; for it is because that ye are cast out, that ye are despised of your brethren because of your exceeding poverty, that ye are brought to a lowliness of heart; for ye are necessarily brought to be humble.

"And now, because ye are compelled to be humble blessed are ye; for a man sometimes, if he is compelled to be humble, seeketh repentance; and now surely, whosoever repenteth shall find mercy; and he that findeth mercy and endureth to the end the same shall be saved.

"And now, as I said unto you, that because ye were compelled to be humble ye were blessed, do ye not suppose that they are more blessed who truly humble themselves because of the word?

"Yea, he that truly humbleth himself, and repenteth of his sins, and endureth to the end, the same shall be blessed—yea, much more blessed than they who are compelled to be

humble because of their exceeding poverty."
(Alma 32:12–15.)

Integrity

The word *integrity* implies oneness and
wholeness. If we have integrity, we have con-
victions, purposes, and values, and we live in
harmony with them. It means that we are as
good as our word. It means that our acts are
consistent with our beliefs, with no guile, pre-
tense, deception, or hypocrisy in our behavior.

Jesus taught and emphasized integrity. I am
struck in the New Testament record by the
intensity of his loathing for hypocrisy. In a long
passage in the Sermon on the Mount, he en-
couraged us to act with pure motives and
singleness of purpose:

*"Take heed that ye do not your alms before
men, to be seen of them: otherwise ye have no
reward of your Father which is in heaven.
Therefore when thou doest thine alms, do not
sound a trumpet before thee, as the hypocrites
do in the synagogues and in the streets, that
they may have glory of men. Verily I say unto
you, They have their reward. But when thou
doest alms, let not thy left hand know what thy*

right hand doeth: that thine alms may be in secret: and thy Father which seeth in secret himself shall reward thee openly.

"And when thou prayest, thou shalt not be as the hypocrites are: for they love to pray standing in the synagogues and in the corners of the streets, that they may be seen of men. Verily I say unto you, They have their reward. But thou, when thou prayest, enter into thy closet, and when thou hast shut thy door, pray to thy Father which is in secret; and thy Father which seeth in secret shall reward thee openly.

"But when ye pray, use not vain repetitions, as the heathen do: for they think that they shall be heard for their much speaking. Be not ye therefore like unto them: for your Father knoweth what things ye have need of, before ye ask him." (Matthew 6:1–8.)

I have always considered it significant that Jesus, to make certain that our love is genuine and not self-seeking, asks us to love our enemies and those who cannot reward us:

"Love your enemies, bless them that curse you, do good to them that hate you, and pray for them which despitefully use you, and persecute you; that ye may be the children of your

Father which is in heaven: for he maketh his sun to rise on the evil and on the good, and sendeth rain on the just and on the unjust. For if ye love them which love you, what reward have ye? do not even the publicans the same?" (Matthew 5:44–46.)

Jesus was unsparing in his condemnation of certain religious practices that some scribes and Pharisees indulged in hypocritically, without sincerity. He warned his listeners to "observe and do" what the Pharisees preached, but "do not ye after their works." He accused them:

"For they bind heavy burdens and grievous to be borne, and lay them on men's shoulders; but they themselves will not move them with one of their fingers. But all their works they do for to be seen of men: they make broad their phylacteries, and enlarge the borders of their garments, and love the uppermost rooms at feasts, and the chief seats in the synagogues, and greetings in the markets, and to be called of men, Rabbi, Rabbi." (Matthew 23:3–7.)

He drove money changers out of the temple because they violated the integrity of the temple as a house of prayer:

"And Jesus went into the temple, and began to cast out them that sold and bought in the temple, and overthrew the tables of the money-changers, and the seats of them that sold doves; and would not suffer that any man should carry any vessel through the temple. And he taught, saying unto them, *Is it not written, My house shall be called of all nations the house of prayer? but ye have made it a den of thieves.*" (Mark 11:15–17.)

The finest contribution Jesus made to the concept of integrity was the quality of his own life. He lived the truth as he perceived it, fearlessly and forthrightly. Believing that he came to accomplish the Resurrection, he endured the pain of his mission and his execution without any attempt to avoid it or to persuade God or humans to alleviate his suffering. Consistent with his own teachings of unconditional love, he asked the Father to forgive those who crucified him.

Integrity is an overarching personal virtue. It includes sincerity, honesty, truthfulness, moral courage, humility, meekness, and repentance. It provides a sense of identity that rises above the trivialities of daily life and gives peace and serenity even during life's vicissitudes.

I have often been inspired by Job, who steadfastly held fast his integrity even when God himself seemed against him. When Bildad asserted God's absolute sovereignty, comparing man to "a worm," Job protested:

"As God liveth, who hath taken away my judgment; and the Almighty, who hath vexed my soul; all the while my breath is in me, and the spirit of God is in my nostrils; my lips shall not speak wickedness, nor my tongue utter deceit. God forbid that I should justify you: till I die I will not remove mine integrity from me. My righteousness I hold fast, and will not let it go: my heart shall not reproach me so long as I live." (Job 27:2–6.)

Job felt assurance in being judged on the basis of his actions as well as his intentions:

"If I have walked with vanity, or if my foot hath hasted to deceit; let me be weighed in an even balance, that God may know mine integrity. If my step hath turned out of the way, and mine heart walked after mine eyes, and if any blot hath cleaved to mine hands; then let me sow, and let another eat; yea, let my offspring be rooted out. . . .

"If I have lifted up my hand against the fatherless, when I saw my help in the gate: then let mine arm fall from my shoulder blade, and mine arm be broken from the bone." (Job 31: 5–8, 21–22.)

We are justly warned against the sin of pride, but I would hope that each of us, like Job, can hold our own integrity with such firmness and lack of self-deception that we, like him, can be "righteous in [our] own eyes." (Job 32:1.) That is a goal worthy of our striving.

LOVE

The central and controlling principle of human existence for Jesus was love, which occupied first and second place among the commandments. Thus, love is the foundation upon which every other religious and ethical principle depends.

"By this shall all men know that ye are my disciples," he said, *"if ye have love one to another."* (John 13:35.)

At the close of his mission, he asked Peter three times, *"Lovest thou me?"* Peter replied,

"Yea, Lord; thou knowest that I love thee." And each time, Jesus responded with a call to serve others out of that love: *"Feed my lambs. . . . Feed my sheep. . . . Feed my sheep."* (John 21:15–17.)

Paul caught the spirit of Jesus when he wrote a stirring eulogy on love to the Corinthians that concludes with the categorical statement: "And now abideth faith, hope, [love], these three; but the greatest of these is [love]." (1 Corinthians 13:13.)

To the Galatians, Paul explained, "For all the law is fulfilled in one word, even in this; Thou shalt love thy neighbour as thyself."

Students of human nature generally agree that a person's most basic need, beyond those needs that insure sheer physical survival, is to be accepted, wanted, and loved. Jesus' concern that we become fully human and realize the potential of our lives springs out of a solid root in the position love has in his ethical and religious thought.

Love for Jesus was both a noun and a verb. It meant that our attitudes and orientations should reflect a concern for the eternal well-being of other human souls and that our behavior should mirror that value. I believe that social isolation is much more a fact of our modern, urban lives than it was of his listeners, and that we therefore have a special challenge in responding to this commandment. I believe that if each of us will listen to our hearts, they will whisper to us of individuals we already know whose needs for love are not being met. Perhaps we will also hear about special populations of the love-hungry to whom our services will be especially beneficial: the homeless, those who are in prison, the mentally or physically handicapped, the terminally ill, neglected or abused children.

My own work has brought me into close contact with the elderly, within whose ranks I now stand. In the Salt Lake Valley alone, there are literally hundreds of them, mostly women, who have neither spouse nor children and who face disability and death alone. When they were younger, keeping neat houses and gardens was to them a great source of pride and self-esteem. Now they sit and watch their homes disintegrate and weeds grow in their yards. I know two women who are legally blind, living on incomes that don't permit them to call a plumber, carpenter, painter, or gardener.

Even those who can hire some of these services are not free from loneliness. I took a box of food from the Salt Lake Food Bank to an elderly widow one winter day. After a friendly visit, I wished her well. She said, "Mr. Bennion, come again, if it's only to say hello." I hope her next visitor feels, as I felt, that the promise of the Savior had been fulfilled for us: *"Where two or three are gathered together in my name, there am I in the midst of them."* (Matthew 18:20.)

Faith

Jesus acknowledged his Father as the source of his beliefs and actions. His was a strong, sensible, and undoubting faith that we live in God's world and that he has a deep concern for our well-being. Whenever I feel lonely or insecure, I like to read the Sermon on the Mount, where he expressed, in beautiful words, his simple and complete trust in the Father:

"Therefore I say unto you, Take no thought for your life, what ye shall eat, or what ye shall drink; nor yet for your body, what ye shall put on. Is not the life more than meat, and the body

than raiment? Behold the fowls of the air: for they sow not, neither do they reap, nor gather into barns; yet your heavenly Father feedeth them. Are ye not much better than they? Which of you by taking thought can add one cubit unto his stature?

"And why take ye thought for raiment? Consider the lilies of the field, how they grow; they toil not, neither do they spin: and yet I say unto you, That even Solomon in all his glory was not arrayed like one of these. Wherefore, if God so clothe the grass of the field, which to day is, and to morrow is cast into the oven, shall he not much more clothe you, O ye of little faith?

"Therefore take no thought, saying, What shall we eat? or, What shall we drink? or, Wherewithal shall we be clothed? (For after all these things do the Gentiles seek:) for your heavenly Father knoweth that ye have need of all these things.

"But seek ye first the kingdom of God, and his righteousness; and all these things shall be added unto you.

"Take therefore no thought for the morrow: for the morrow shall take thought for the things

of itself. Sufficient unto the day is the evil thereof." (Matthew 6:25–34.)

There is a great deal of peace for me in these words. They clarify my priorities, simplify my perspective, and ring with reassurance.

Another favorite passage of scripture that illuminates the nature of faith is the fascinating conversation that grew out of an encounter Jesus had with a concerned father who had a very disturbed son. He told the man, *"If thou canst believe, all things are possible to him that believeth.*

"And straightway the father of the child cried out, and said with tears, Lord, I believe; help thou mine unbelief.

"When Jesus saw that the people came running together, he rebuked the foul spirit, saying unto him, *Thou dumb and deaf spirit, I charge thee, come out of him, and enter no more into him.*

"And the spirit cried, and rent him sore, and came out of him: and he was as one dead; insomuch that many said, He is dead. But Jesus took him by the hand, and lifted him up; and he arose." (Mark 9:23–27.)

It is the cry of the father that resonates in

my own heart. In the presence of the Master, the father believed; but upon reflection, he realized that he did not always have faith. My faith, like his, is not always free of doubt. I, too, on occasion, cry, "Lord, help thou mine unbelief."

Many people are disturbed when they find doubts intruding into their faith, particularly young people who, as a natural stage in their maturation, are questioning the simple faith of their childhood. I try to point out to them two facts: Jesus did not rebuke the father for his unbelief, and the father confessed his unbelief to the Savior in the context of asking for help. I believe that our Heavenly Father is pleased with such confessions. What could make for healthier growth than expressing doubts in a context of faith? Indifference, it seems to me, is far deadlier to faith than doubt.

It is not easy in our time to maintain a simple faith in God. Perhaps it never was easy. As I have grown older, I no longer see faith as an answer-finding instrument, if you will. I still have many questions. Some of them are questions that have perplexed me from my youth, while others are questions that have come as

I have learned to ask different questions of life. But at the heart of my faith is a strong and solid core: God sees life from a different perspective than we do. What is important for us is to believe that God lives, that he has a purpose in his dealings with us, and that the principles Jesus taught have both eternal and temporal value. With such faith, I am more willing to also develop the virtue of patience.

Humility, integrity, love, and *faith.* Even though our discussion of these four basic principles that Jesus taught and lived has been brief, it is remarkable to me how they interface and support one another. A person cannot have integrity without humility, because only humility can provide the self-acceptance to know one's central values and the freedom from fear to express them. On the other hand, without integrity one's humility is actually hypocrisy, lacking in honesty and sincerity.

Certainly one cannot love a neighbor without having a good measure of integrity. Love has no motive beyond itself. "Love," so-called, that stems from fear, duty, or a desire to get to the celestial kingdom is not really love at all, and the acts of such "love" are poisoned by self-interest.

A person of humility, integrity, and faith needs a supreme, unifying purpose in life. Love of God and of other beings provides such a goal. Jesus' philosophy of life hangs together beautifully. Humility and faith relate people to God and Christ; integrity and love are essential in human relations. All four principles enrich one another, illustrating the genius of Jesus, the master teacher, and the power of his perfect life.

Chapter 5

Jesus' Art of Teaching

Teaching is an art, not a science. I speak as someone who has labored long to learn its secrets, only to find it as mysterious as it is magical. In this realm, as in so many others, Jesus is my master. He was an artist, not only in the substance of his teaching but also in his manner and forms.

As a teacher, Jesus is most famous for the parables he created. Parables are stories taken from life, crafted by Jesus' imagination and insights, that illustrate gospel principles. Stories are remembered even when abstract reasoning, though clearly understood, is forgotten. Parables have been described as earthly stories with heavenly meanings. They are a particularly good form for the purpose that seemed to dominate Jesus' teaching — to transmit principles rather than rules or mere information. Life is dynamic; conditions change in almost infinite variety. Rules become outmoded; principles do not.

The Gospels of Matthew and Luke record many parables. Two of my favorites are the parable of the good Samaritan and the parable of the prodigal son, both of which preach eloquently and irresistibly the value of other human beings. When a man asked Jesus, "Who is my neighbour?" Jesus responded with a story so real and true to life that it could have happened exactly as he told it. But using imagination and casting the despised Samaritan as the good neighbor, he made his point with absorbing interest, clarity, and originality.

The parable of the prodigal son illustrated the rich human interest Jesus included in many of his parables. Many families have a son or daughter who seeks independence by leaving the family home and even rejecting the family's values. To have the father celebrate his son's return was a very effective way for Jesus to teach the Pharisees the worth of souls. How natural, too, for an older brother to be envious and judgmental.

Another characteristic of Jesus' parables was the concreteness of his language. He talked about things his hearers could touch and see, using simple, vigorous verbs and clearly described behavior, as we see in this example:

"A sower went out to sow his seed: and as he sowed, some fell by the way side; and it was trodden down, and the fowls of the air devoured it. And some fell upon a rock; and as soon as it was sprung up, it withered away, because it lacked moisture. And some fell among thorns; and the thorns sprang up with it, and choked it. And other fell on good ground, and sprang up, and bare fruit an hundredfold. And when he had said these things, he cried, He that hath ears to hear, let him hear." (Luke 8:5–8)

A friend once commented, "You have been a teacher all your life. What have you learned from Jesus about how to teach religion?" I haven't been able to duplicate Jesus' wonderful art of creating parables and proverbs, but I have tried to emulate his teaching art in five specific ways.

1. A trait that I prize very highly in Jesus' teaching and which I have tried to emulate in my own is his positiveness. Instead of "thou shalt not," he said "thou shalt" and "blessed are . . . " To the lawyer who heard the good Samaritan parable and was forced to admit the answer to the question, Jesus responded not with mockery or by gloating, but with the simple, friendly admonition, *"Go, and do thou likewise."* Negative admonitions have their place, but positive statements win readier responses from beings whose free agency is the most fundamental fact of their nature. Also, we are *doers*, and a negative admonition is an order not to do. Positive injunctions have wider applications, I have found.

2. I see Jesus as very wise, even brilliant, in his interaction with people, including those with ulterior motives. I am not sure that such insight is always available to mere mortals, but I believe that humility might frequently be a good substitute. Rather than feeling obliged to share all of our wisdom, we could follow the model of Jesus, who frequently answered a

question by asking another question. He made people think, clarify their motives, explore options for themselves, and prize the insights they gained thereby.

For example, when such a person asked if it were lawful to pay tribute to Caesar, thus acknowledging the legal lordship of the country's hated rulers, Jesus called for a coin, asked his questioner whose image it bore, and thus led him into identifying the image as Caesar's: *"Render therefore unto Caesar the things which are Caesar's; and unto God the things that are God's."* (Matthew 22:21.)

As a teacher, I truly enjoy the process of helping people become their own teachers, rather than passively receiving instructions. Jesus' use of judicious questions is an effective way of accomplishing this end.

3. He taught not lessons but people. A student complained to me once that she was having a terrible time teaching her Sunday School class of twelve-year-olds. I asked, "What do you have in mind as you prepare your lesson?"

She replied, "How to keep the kids quiet while I give it."

I was tempted to tell her that the best way

to do that was to gag and hog-tie them. But remembering Jesus' way, I asked her if she thought it might be more effective to teach not the lessons, but the twelve-year-olds. What did she know about them? their interests? their family backgrounds? their problems? How did they teach each other? What kinds of things did they seem to want to learn?

She became quite interested in this approach, which eliminated the built-in contest between what they were doing and what she wanted them to do. I believe she saw the point I was trying to make: that the purpose of Sunday School is not to teach the gospel to people but rather to teach people the gospel. Thanks to Jesus, I always try to teach people, and to have them leave the classroom with increased faith, humility, love, or insight.

4. Jesus taught single ideas. He drove home a single point in each of his parables and discussions. That is why they are still memorable and applicable.

I learned from Jesus that a good lesson is one idea, organized and illustrated, and readily—even vividly—applicable to the lives of the class members. Too often in our classes, we try to cover a multitude of ideas or many aspects of a basic theme. We take a shotgun approach. A good lesson should be like a rifle shot, in which the teacher develops one very specific idea or principle with the insights of the class.

For example, instead of discussing all aspects of prayer in one lesson, why not treat a single question, such as, "When have you had reason to pray with great meaning and motivation?" This is a need we all have. Class members will think first not of rules, but of their own experiences. And in the sharing, they will stimulate and enlighten each other—and the teacher.

5. Jesus taught fundamental principles, not isolated facts or theories that do not lead directly to edification. I have listened to many discussions, some of them heated, on the nature of eternal progression, the location of the Ten Tribes, or what Joseph Smith may have meant on such and such a point. As a teacher, I believe that the time of a class is too precious to spend on anything but the most important principles that teach us how to live our lives. The accumulation of opinions about historical or future points on which we lack adequate

information to make informed decisions is not, in my opinion, the most valuable way to spend an hour together.

I suspect that Jesus, like most great teachers, truly loved not only those he taught and the concepts he conveyed but also the very process of teaching. What else is teaching besides the shared search for greater truth and understanding through the characteristics that make us most human—through reason, through discourse, through sympathy, and through making connections so that our vision expands and we see relationships that we had not hitherto guessed? In fact, that's not a bad definition of heaven, too, as far as I'm concerned.

Chapter 6

Jesus and the Atonement

Thus far we have talked about Jesus' ethical and humanitarian qualities, his superb teaching gifts, his values, and the place of humility, integrity, love, and faith in his religious principles. His unique position as both an emissary and an exemplary prophet gives him authority. For all of these reasons, he merits our discipleship.

But we have said nothing as yet about his divinity—nothing about our eternal relationship to him, his atonement, and his redemption. It may be possible to give him the reasoned obedience due to a great ethical and moral teacher, but for me, my discipleship stems from my conviction of his divinity. What does his godhood mean to my worship?

Let me suggest the meaning I read in John 3:16–17:

"For God so loved the world, that he gave his only begotten Son, that whosoever believeth in him should not perish, but have everlasting life. For God sent not his Son into the world to condemn the world; but that the world through him might be saved."

Christ's eternal mission on behalf of human beings was fulfilled in his atonement. Literally the word means at-one-ment, signifying that we should be in harmony with God, at one with him and his Son. If we are to be at one with Deity, *we* must change — not God. We must overcome the limitations in our lives, for they have no counterpart in the life of God.

What human conditions deny us unity with God? What circumstances must we overcome to be one with him? What must we be saved from to obtain salvation? I believe we must overcome three things to be at one with God: mortality, ignorance, and sin.

Overcoming mortality, quite simply and flatly, lies beyond our powers. Despite medical advances, despite care to one's diet, exercise, and health, death awaits us all. Here, in the immutable and inescapable fact of our own demise, we must either reach out to Christ for help or face it alone.

One of Christ's self-announced missions on earth was to conquer death, making it possible for each person who has ever lived to pass into an immortal, resurrected state. As the first mortal to be resurrected, Christ is in a position to promise all human beings that they will rise from the grave with a tangible, perfected, immortal body. In Alma we read: "The soul shall be restored to the body, and the body to the soul; yea, and every limb and joint shall be restored to its body; yea, even a hair of the head shall not be lost; but all things shall be restored to their proper and perfect frame." (Alma 40:23.)

How the Resurrection takes place, and exactly how Christ effects it, we do not understand. We do understand that it is universal and irresistible, "for as in Adam all die, even so in Christ shall all be made alive." (1 Corinthians 15:22.) The Resurrection appeals to us as a miracle, a pure gift of grace from the Son of God.

When Socrates was condemned to death, his friends offered to help him escape death, but he refused. As Plato records that final night with his friends, Socrates said that no harm could come to a good man in death because death was either the best night's sleep a person ever had, undisturbed by dreams or nightmares, or the passage to another world where justice reigns and where one can converse with great individuals who have gone before.

I have always appreciated Socrates' curiosity and his calmness; and even if there were no immortality, this life would still be of great value while it lasted. But such a condition would be sad. To have life end just when we have come to know and enjoy it is a tragedy indeed. Jesus is my basis for believing in eternal life. I know that his ethical and practical religious teachings are true, and they strengthen my faith in what he said about the Resurrection.

We receive, then, the Resurrection as pure gift, as something we simply cannot do for ourselves. The other two conditions, ignorance and sin, are direct responsibilities of our own,

though Christ stands ready to help us, to redeem our incapacity, and to complete our de-
ficiencies. Ignorance is not a sin unless we
willfully refuse to learn, but it is a limitation
almost as serious as sin. *"And ye shall know
the truth,"* Jesus promised, *"and the truth shall
make you free."* (John 8:32.) In his gospel, we
find the means of overcoming ignorance. As
human beings, we have rational and insatiable
minds. We are eternal intelligences, and the
acquisition of truth is a desire that is built into
our nature. Christ came to earth to teach us
the truth.

One of the most important things we need
to learn is what are the attributes of God. Christ
came to earth to reveal to us the character of
God. He is the revelation of God to human
beings, teaching us by precept and example
the meaning of faith, humility, integrity, and
love.

We do not learn about these divine attributes by mere reason or by reading the scriptures. We must learn them experientially, by
living them. This process may take eons, and
mortality is a crucial part of that process.

The third thing we must overcome is sin,

which binds us by using our inborn free agency to make wrong decisions. Knowingly, either by commission or by omission, when we sin we act contrary to what we know is right. Jesus describes both ignorance and sin in commenting to the Pharisees: *"If ye were blind, ye should have no sin: but now ye say, We see; therefore your sin remaineth."* (John 9:41.) A person may act in ignorance, but he or she cannot sin in ignorance. And all of us, the scriptures testify, are sinners. We fail to measure up to our knowledge of the right.

Knowing the truth is a great step toward freedom from sin, followed by applying our agency to make correct choices. But even our best efforts will fall short of achieving such freedom without the aid of Christ.

What is Christ's relationship to the sins of humankind? There is only one way to overcome sin in our lives, and that is to repent, which means to eradicate it from our thinking and action. Christ helps us repent in two ways. First, his teachings and the example of his perfect life help us recognize that we are sinners until we repent of our wrongdoing. Second, he gives us faith unto repentance, motivating us to change our desires and behavior.

For me, one of the most powerful motives is his love for me, which in turn calls out my love for him. Christ loves us so much that our evildoing causes him to suffer. I remember as a child that there were some forms of naughtiness and mischief that I simply would not participate in because I knew that it would hurt my mother. Similarly, for believing Christians, the realization that we are causing our Savior pain is, in itself, a vigorous motivation to repent. I have sometimes flinched as I have read King Benjamin's testimony to his people: "And lo, he shall suffer temptations, and pain of body, hunger, thirst, and fatigue, even more than man can suffer, except it be unto death; for behold, blood cometh from every pore, so great shall be his anguish for the wickedness and the abominations of his people." (Mosiah 3:7.)

Another way in which Christ motivates change is through the power of his life and teaching. The inspiration of a better way leads us to emulate, even in our limited and broken ways, that perfection. This motive may be particularly true of someone who has tasted the bitterness of a life of sin through wrongdoing.

When I was a missionary, a man confessed a serious sin to me. He was in a very unhappy frame of mind, guilty and tormented by his conscience. He was a teacher in the Aaronic Priesthood, so I asked him, "Will you accept an assignment to prepare the sacrament table each week?"

He was startled. "Do you think I'm worthy?"

"No," I answered, "none of us are, but I believe Jesus would be pleased if you would render him this service."

The man came to me in a few months and said, "I'm a new person. My thoughts are where they ought to be."

Thinking of Jesus and rendering a specific service for him enabled this man to change his feelings from regret and depression to hope and joy. I guessed that this might be so since I had observed in my own life that I committed very few sins while thinking about my Savior or serving him.

Jesus helps us repent by promising forgiveness to those who truly repent. He affirms the teaching of Ezekiel:

"But if the wicked will turn from all his sins that he hath committed, and keep all my statutes, and do that which is lawful and right, he shall surely live, he shall not die. All his transgressions that he hath committed, they shall not be mentioned unto him: in his righteousness that he hath done he shall live. Have I any pleasure at all that the wicked should die? saith the Lord God: and not that he should return from his ways, and live?" (Ezekiel 18: 21–23.)

The New Testament contains many thrilling accounts of Jesus cutting directly and powerfully through the torment, guilt, and frustration of a sinner to forgive him or her. There are no elaborate contracts or negotiations that balance so much repentance against so much sin. Jesus simply and cleanly frees the person from all of that tangle, thus prompting Paul to remind the Colossians later about the importance of "forbearing one another, and forgiving one another, . . . even as Christ forgave you, so also do ye." (Colossians 3:13.)

In short, Christ makes us aware of our sins, moves us to repent from them, and promises forgiveness when we do. These are acts of grace and love; they empower us to overcome sin and its destructive role in our lives.

The apostle Paul and the other prophets believed that Jesus did one more thing for our sins, and their testimony has become part of mine. They believed that he took upon himself the sins of those who repent, that he suffered for our sins so that his mercy could satisfy the demands of justice.

I do not understand the mechanisms of redemption, and I am not sure that legal arguments of retribution and restitution adequately capture that process; but the prophets imply that we live in a world of law. When the laws are broken, somehow they must be made good or be satisfied. Jesus paid the price of our sins, according to this view. When he visited the Nephites, he said:

"Behold, I am the light and the life of the world; and I have drunk out of that bitter cup which the Father hath given me, and have glorified the Father in taking upon me the sins of the world, in the which I have suffered the will of the Father in all things from the beginning." (3 Nephi 11:11.)

Just as we cannot understand in mortality

how the Resurrection is made possible, neither do we know why or how Christ "pays" for our sins. But there is plenty that we do understand: the nature of sin, its destructive consequences, our need to repent, and the assurance of forgiveness if we do. We can be grateful for Christ's grace, which, indeed, is "sufficient" (2 Corinthians 12:9) both for overcoming death on our behalf and, united with our best efforts, for overcoming ignorance and sin within us.

Christ deserves the title "Son of God" by the beauty and perfection of his life and teachings. However, this title is not merely a tribute to his goodness, but a literal description of his divinity, according to the scriptures. He was human by birth, but more than human. In the scriptures Mary was told by an angel, "The Holy Ghost shall come upon thee, and the power of the Highest shall overshadow thee: therefore also that holy thing which shall be born of thee shall be called the Son of God." (Luke 1:35.)

Facing his crucifixion, Jesus testified: *"Therefore doth my Father love me, because I lay down my life, that I might take it again. No man taketh it from me, but I lay it down of myself. I have power to lay it down, and I have power to take it again."* (John 10:17–18.)

Once again, a great mystery surrounds how Jesus received his divine nature, but we can accept the fact in that mystery, believing that he undertook his mission of redemption on behalf of humankind. His life and death are evidence of his boundless grace as our redeemer from death, ignorance, and sin.

I am not a poet. I envy those who have the ability to cast the deeply felt thoughts of their heart into eloquent and beautiful forms. The thought of the Atonement stirs feelings of gratitude and awe that I cannot begin to express, but I believe that my favorite sacrament hymn, "I Stand All Amazed," does a fair job of capturing these feelings:

> I stand all amazed at the love Jesus
>   offers me,
> Confused at the grace that so fully
>   he proffers me.
> I tremble to know that for me
>   he was crucified,
> That for me, a sinner, he suffered,
>   he bled and died.

I marvel that he would descend
  from his throne divine
To rescue a soul so rebellious
  and proud as mine,
That he should extend his great love
  unto such as I,
Sufficient to own, to redeem,
  and to justify.

I think of his hands pierced and
  bleeding to pay the debt,
Such mercy, such love, and devotion
  can I forget?
No, no, I will praise and adore
  at the mercy seat,
Until at the glorified throne I kneel
  at his feet.

—*Hymns,* 1985, no. 193